Introduction To Excel VBA Macros Using Visual Basic

Explanations, Sample Code, and Detailed Practice Assignment with Full Solution

L Castelluzzo

ISBN-10: 1686765339
ISBN-13: 978-1686765339

Independently published

Preface

This book teaches the reader how to begin using Visual Basic code to write and execute customized macros in Microsoft Excel. Topics include: variables, worksheets, spreadsheet files, cell formulas, relative referencing, copying and pasting, finding cells with data, setting up a range for cell referencing, pivot tables, cell formatting, and much more.

The intention is to teach the reader how to perform regular tasks in Excel using Visual Basic code instead of the regular manual method. This will allow the reader to perform their work thousands of times faster with no effort once they have finished writing their macro. All of the code in this book will be available for download from the Internet at:

https://sites.google.com/view/questions-with-solutions/excel-vba-macro-code

. The code that has been provided in this book has been written as generically as possible in order to allow it to be used with minimal modification. It is not necessary for the user to memorize code, but it is very useful for the user to build a library of snippets which they tend to use most frequently and to become very familiar with their most commonly used macro code.

This book also provides an opportunity to put this new code to work in the form of an assignment which involves writing a full macro. Details and instructions are provided, and the full solution is provided as well.

Introduction to Excel VBA Macros Using Visual Basic

WHERE TO BEGIN

While using Microsoft Excel, the keyboard shortcut is Alt-F11 to begin writing code for a macro.

Alternatively,
Excel 2007: Click: Developer > Visual Basic
Excel 2016: Click: View > Macros > View Macros

Input any macro name and click Create.
Click: Insert > Module
Begin typing the code in the large white section on the right.

All macros begin with:
```
Sub MacroName()
```

All macros end with:
```
End Sub
```

Text that is placed after an apostrophe within a given line is ignored by the macro. This allows the user to insert commentary which explains the code in layman's terms, and all of this text which is after the apostrophe appears green in the Visual Basic macro editor.

The code in this book is intended to be copied into the Visual Basic window, and altered to suit the specific situation. The `Courier font` is used to indicate the code that can be copied and pasted into Visual Basic. This includes the commentary after the apostrophe which explains each line, and which should be included with the code in order to make it much easier to review and adjust in the future.

Please note that if a line of code is displayed on two or more lines, it important to treat it as a single long line of code when copying it into the macro. In this book, each separate line of code is separated by a blank line.

All variable names are underlined, and **bold** text is used to indicate which parts of the code will need to be altered according to the situation where it is used. The code will not appear bold or underlined after it is input into the macro editor.

VARIABLES

Variables are used to temporarily store snippets of information, which are used in different worksheets and in different formulas. The reason why variables are used is because the spreadsheet changes as a macro is running, and so variables allow certain information to stay the same or change as needed. One way to understand a variable is to visualize it as a box with a label on it, and the information is like a sheet of paper with writing on it, which is placed into the box while the macro is running.

It is common practice that all variables which will be used are declared at the beginning of the macro, or if not at the beginning, then they need to be declared before the variable is used. Variables can be given any name and the name can be as short as one letter long, as long as there are no spaces. It is best to use a name which is concise and which represents the information that is being stored.

```
Dim VariableName As VariableType ' Declare
the variable according to the info it holds
```

The variable types allow the macro to handle the variable according to the situation.
`Long` = numbers
`String` = text
`Workbook` = spreadsheet file
`Worksheet` = worksheet tab
`Range` = a range of cells

Once a variable has been declared, it is ready to be used to store information.

VARIABLES THAT STORE A STRING OF TEXT

When a string of text is being used or stored, it needs to be within quotation marks.

```
' Declare CustomerName to be a variable
which holds text

Dim CustomerName as String

' Store the word Michael in the CustomerName
variable

CustomerName = "Michael"
```

The amperstand (&) is used to concatenate or combine information side by side, such as strings of text.

If a string variable is being used or adjusted, the name of the variable itself cannot be within quotation marks.

```
' Store the word Smith by appending it to
whatever is currently stored in the
CustomerName variable. In this case, the
variable will contain Michael Smith. A space
was included inside the quotation marks, so
that the name would appear as 2 separate
words.

CustomerName = CustomerName & " Smith"
```

VARIABLES THAT STORE A NUMBER

` Declare AccountBalance to be a variable
that holds numbers

Dim AccountBalance as Long

` Store the number 10,000 in the
AccountBalance variable

AccountBalance = **10000**

AccountBalance = **AccountBalance - 6000** `
Decrease the AccountBalance variable by 6000

VARIABLES THAT STORE WORKBOOK NAMES

```
' Declare BankChart as a variable that
stores a spreadsheet's filename

Dim BankChartsWB as Workbook

' Store the name of the spreadsheet file
called Banking.xlsx as a variable.

Set BankChartsWB = Workbooks("Banking.xlsx")
```

By setting up this variable, it will be easier to read and write the code. This is because going forward, instead of typing `Workbooks("Banking.xlsm")`, it will only be necessary to reference this file by typing `BankChartsWB`.

```
' Close workbook without saving

BankChartsWB.Close SaveChanges:=False
```

ActiveWorkbook is a quick way to refer to whichever spreadsheet file is currently activated, without indicating the name of the file or the variable that stores the name of the file.

```
' Save the spreadsheet that is active

ActiveWorkbook.Save

' Close the spreadsheet that is active

ActiveWorkbook.Close
```

VARIABLES THAT STORE WORKSHEET (TAB) NAMES

```
Dim AccountTab as Worksheet

Set AccountTab = Workbooks
("Banking.xlsx").Worksheets("Account")
```

By setting up this variable, it will be easier to read and write the code. This is because going forward, instead of typing "`Workbooks("Banking.xlsx").Worksheets("Account")`", it will only be necessary to reference this tab by typing `AccountTab`.

WORKSHEET TABS

The word "tab" is commonly used to describe what Microsoft Excel refers to as a "worksheet". Even though Excel refers to them as worksheets or sheets, and never refers to them as tabs, this book uses the term "worksheet" and "tab" interchangeably.

In many cases, it is important to activate the relevant tab before the code is input for that tab. This is because the macro might be unintentionally initiated while viewing a tab that is not applicable to the code, and if this happens the macro will blindly apply the code to whichever tab happens to be activated (ie displayed) at that point in time.

Activating a worksheet is the equivalent to clicking on a tab with the mouse. It is possible to write each line of code in a way which indicates the tab that is being worked affected, however when a block of code is working on a specific tab, it is a good habit to include code which activates the tab, and if the tab is already activated, there is no harm in activating it again.

```
' Activate a spreadsheet file

Workbooks("Filename.xlsx").Activate

' Activate a spreadsheet file

WorkbookVariableName.Activate

' Activate a worksheet tab

Workbooks("Filename.xlsx").Worksheets(
"TabName").Activate

' Activate a worksheet tab

WorksheetVariableName.Activate
```

It is not necessary to activate a workbook. By activating the tab, the workbook which is included in the code is automatically included in the activation.

ActiveSheet is a quick way to refer to whichever worksheet tab is currently activated, without indicating the name of the tab or the variable that stores the name of the tab.

```
' Unhide all hidden cells

ActiveSheet.ShowAllData

' Expand all grouped cells to the most
expanded level (8th) level

ActiveSheet.ShowLevels RowLevels:=8,
ColumnLevels:=8

' Insert a tab after the tab called TabName

Sheets.Add After:=Sheets("TabName")
```

```vba
' Insert a blank tab after the 3rd tab in the
spreadsheet

Sheets.Add After:=Sheets(3)

' Insert a blank tab after the last tab

Sheets.Add After:=Sheets(Sheets.Count)

' Duplicate the tab, and place the copy
after the worksheet called TabName

ActiveSheet.Copy After:=Sheets("TabName")

' Duplicate the tab, and place the copy
after the 2nd tab

ActiveSheet.Copy After:=Sheets(2)

' Duplicate the tab, and place the copy
after the last worksheet

ActiveSheet.Copy After:=Sheets(Sheets.Count)

' Rename the active tab to NewTabName

ActiveSheet.Name = "NewTabName"
```

CELL IDENTIFICATION

Range indicates the address of one cell or a group of cells. If the Range contains a cell address, then it requires quotation marks.

`Range ("A1")` or `Range ("A1:C3")`

The Cells() function allows the user to refer to a cell using numbers instead of a cell address. This is very helpful because it allows the user to specify a cell using numeric variables. One cell can be specified by typing:

`Cells (RowNumber, ColumnNumber)`

`Cells (5, 10)` is the equivalent of `Range ("J5")`

More than one cell can be specified by combining the range and cells functions, as long as the underlined variables have already been defined as numeric variables.

`Range (Cells (1stCellRow, 1stCellColumn), Cells (2ndCellRow, 2ndCellColumn))`

`Range (Cells (1, 2), Cells (10, 3))` is the equivalent of `Range ("B1:C10")`

If the code is referring to a range on the active worksheet, then it is not necessary to specify which workbook or worksheet. To refer to a range on the active worksheet:
`Range ("A1")`

It is possible to refer to a range on a specific worksheet without activating the worksheet:

```
Workbooks("Filename.xlsx").Worksheets("TabName").Range("A1")
```

or if the tab has already been declared and input into a worksheet variable:

```
TabVariableName.Range("A1")
```

ActiveCell is a quick way to refer to whichever cell is currently activated, without indicating the range or the variable that stores the range of the cell.

```
ActiveCell
```

CELL SELECTION

The code will result in an error if a range is defined but nothing is done with the range. It is necessary that the user combines one of the above methods of indicating a range with an action.

Typing `.Select` after a cell or range instructs the macro to select those cells. It is the equivalent of clicking on a cell or group of cells.

```
Activesheet.Range("A1").Select

Activesheet.Cells(2,3).Select

Range("D2:Y2").Select

' Selects cells B1 to C10

Range(Cells(1,2),Cells(10,3)).Select
```

The following code is the equivalent of pressing the arrow buttons to move the cursor.

```
' Move the cursor one cell upwards

Selection.Offset(-1, 0).Select

' Move the cursor one cell downwards

Selection.Offset(1, 0).Select

' Move the cursor one cell to the left

Selection.Offset(0, -1).Select

' Move the cursor one cell to the right

Selection.Offset(0, 1).Select
```

CELL CONTENTS – READING AND MODIFYING

Typing `.Value` after a cell or range instructs the macro to obtain the contents of the cell. It is the equivalent of looking at the contents of a cell.

```
' Save the word Michael in cell A1

Range("A1").Value = "Michael"

'Append the word Smith to the text that is
already in cell A1

Range("A1").Value = Range("A1").Value  & "
Smith"

' Save cell A1 into the FullName variable

FullName = Range("A1").Value

' Decrease a cell value by one.

Range("A1").Value = Range("A1").Value - 1

' Increase a cell value by one.

Range("A1").Value = Range("A1").Value + 1
```

CELL CONTENTS - DELETION

Typing `.ClearContents` after a cell or range instructs the macro to erase the cell contents

Typing `.ClearFormats` after a cell or range instructs the macro to remove all cell formatting

```
'Delete all blank rows

Range("A1:Z99").SpecialCells(xlCellTypeBlank
s).EntireRow.Delete

'Delete all non-numeric rows

Range("A1:Z99").SpecialCells(xlCellTypeConst
ants, 2).EntireRow.Delete

'Delete all rows that contain errors

Range("A1:Z99").SpecialCells(xlConstants,
xlErrors).EntireRow.Delete

'Remove duplicates from column 1 or A in the
range of cells from A1 to A99, which is a
range that does not include a header row

Range("A1:A99").RemoveDuplicates Columns:=1,
Header:=xlNo
```

CELL CONTENTS - COPY & PASTE

Before copying cells to the clipboard, it is necessary to first select the cells.

```
' Select all of the cells from A1 to B10

Range("A1:B10").Select

'Copy the selected cells to the clipboard.
This is like pressing CTRL+C.

Selection.Copy

' Move the cursor to the specific cell,
which is cell C50
```

Before pasting the contents of the clipboard into a cell, it is necessary to first select the cell where the contents will go.

```
Range("C50").Select

'Paste the clipboard contents into the cell,
like pressing CTRL+V.

Activesheet.Paste

'Paste Values

Selection.PasteSpecial Paste:=xlPasteValues,
Operation:=xlNone, SkipBlanks:=False,
Transpose:=False

'Paste Formulas

Selection.PasteSpecial Paste:
=xlPasteFormulas, Operation:=xlNone,
SkipBlanks:=False, Transpose:=False

  'Paste Cell Formats

Selection.PasteSpecial
```

```
Paste:=xlPasteFormats, Operation:=xlNone,
SkipBlanks:=False, Transpose:=False
```

After pasting the contents of the clipboard, Microsoft Excel will maintain an animated dashed line (which resemble and are sometimes referred to as "ants") to indicate that the copied data is still selected. If this is not removed, then the macro will be interrupted by a dialogue box which asks if the user would like to delete the contents of the clipboard. To avoid this, the following line of code should be used to de-select the copied data:

```
' Remove clipboard cut/copy border (aka
"ants")

Application.CutCopyMode = False
```

CELL CONTENTS - FORMATTING

```
' Apply bold font to the selected cell(s)

Selection.Font.Bold = True

Selection.Style = "Comma" ' Display numbers
with commas to indicate thousands, millions,
etc as well as two decimal points

' Apply text wrap format to selected cell(s)

Selection.WrapText = True

'Format numbers to show commas, show zeros
as dashes, and have negatives in brackets

Selection.NumberFormat = "_(* #,##0_);_(*
(#,##0);""-"";_(@_)"
```

```vba
' Change the colour of the text in the
selected cell(s) to red

With Selection.Font

    .Color = -16776961

    .TintAndShade = 0

End With


' Change the cell alignment to bottom,
unmerge cells, and wrap text

With Selection

    .HorizontalAlignment = xlGeneral

    .VerticalAlignment = xlBottom

    .WrapText = True

    .ShrinkToFit = False

    .MergeCells = False

End With
```

CELL SHADING aka FILL

```
' Apply orange fill to the cell selection

With Selection.Interior

    .Pattern = xlSolid

    .PatternColorIndex = xlAutomatic

    .Color = 49407

    .TintAndShade = 0

    .PatternTintAndShade = 0

End With
```

CELL BORDERS

```
' Insert cell borders to the top of the cell selection

With Selection.Borders(xlEdgeTop)

    .LineStyle = xlContinuous

    .ColorIndex = 0

    .TintAndShade = 0

    .Weight = xlThin

End With
```

```vba
' Insert cell borders to the bottom of the
cell selection

With Selection.Borders(xlEdgeBottom)

    .LineStyle = xlContinuous

    .ColorIndex = 0

    .TintAndShade = 0

    .Weight = xlThin

End With



' Remove all borders from selected cells

Selection.Borders(xlDiagonalDown).LineStyle
= xlNone

Selection.Borders(xlDiagonalUp).LineStyle =
xlNone

Selection.Borders(xlEdgeLeft).LineStyle =
xlNone

Selection.Borders(xlEdgeRight).LineStyle =
xlNone

Selection.Borders(xlInsideVertical).LineStyl
e = xlNone

Selection.Borders(xlInsideHorizontal).LineSt
yle = xlNone
```

GROUPING DATA

```vba
' Expand all grouped columns & rows

ActiveSheet.Outline.ShowLevels RowLevels:=8,
ColumnLevels:=8

' Collapse all grouped columns &  rows
ActiveSheet.Outline.ShowLevels RowLevels:=1,
ColumnLevels:=1
```

DATA FILTERS

' Place an autofilter on the cell selection, or remove it if there already is one

```
Selection.AutoFilter
```

' Filter this range of cells to only show rows with a "1" in the 9th column.

```
ActiveSheet.Range("A1:Z99").AutoFilter
Field:=9, Criteria1:="1"
```

' From cell A1 to A99, select only the visible cells which are not filtered out.

```
ActiveSheet.Range(Cells(1, 1), Cells(99,
1)).SpecialCells(xlCellTypeVisible).Select
```

' If this row has been filtered to be invisible, then...

```
If Rows(1).EntireRow.Hidden Then
```

' Temporarily ignore errors, such as if there's no filter

```
   On Error Resume Next
```

' Unfilter any filtered data

```
   ActiveSheet.ShowAllData
```

' Resume the regular error procedure ie stop for any bugs in the code

```
   On Error GoTo 0
```

```
EndIf
```

CELL FORMULAS

```
' Add cells A1 to A99
```

When coding a cell to have a formula with absolute references, the cell address is normally used

```
Cells(RowNumber, ColumnNumber).Formula =
"=SUM(A1:A99)"
```

When coding a cell to have a formula with relative references, a negative number in the square brackets means "upwards" for rows and "to the left" for columns. A positive number in the square brackets means "downwards" for rows and "to the right" for columns.

```
' Add the amounts from the cell that is in
the same row and 5 columns to the left, to
the cell that is 4 rows below and 2 columns
to the left of the cell with this formula.
Note: R[+0]C[-5] can be coded as RC[-5]
```

```
Cells(RowNumber, ColumnNumber).FormulaR1C1 =
"=SUM(RC[-5]:R[+4]C[-2])"
```

```
' Hard return (aka new line) within a string
of text in a cell
```

```
Chr(13) & Chr(10)
```

```
' Use the LEFT() function to obtain the
leftmost character, which is the column
letter, from the cell address and stores the
letter in the underlined string variable
```

```
ColumnLetter = Left(SearchRange.Address
(RowAbsolute:=false, Columnabsolute:=False),
1)
```

This string variable can be then combined with any other formula, such as in the following example:

```
' Add the amounts from row 1 of the column
that is defined by the variable to cell Z99

Cells(7, 4).Formula = "=SUM(" & ColumnLetter
& "1:Z99)"
```

Chr(39) is another way of writing an apostrophe. Typing an actual apostrophe in a macro confuses the software by making it think that the programmer is trying to input commentary.

Chr(34) is another way of writing quotation marks. Typing actual quotation marks in a macro confuses the software by making it think that the programmer is trying to input a string of text into the code rather than into a formula.

INDIRECT FUNCTION

The following code sets up cells to contain cell ranges, which will then be used by the INDIRECT() function.

```
Dim RangeOfCells, RangeOfSum, Filename,
DataTabname As String

Dim FirstRowOfData, LastRowOfData as Long

RangeOfCells = Chr(39) & "[" & FileName &
"]" & DataTabName & Chr(39) & "!$A$" &
FirstRowOfData & ":$A$" & LastRowOfData

RangeOfSum = Chr(39) & "[" & FileName & "]"
& DataTabName & Chr(39) & "!$B$" &
FirstRowOfData & ":$B$" & LastRowOfData

Range("D11").Value = RangeOfCells

Range("F11").Value = RangeOfSum

Range("G23").Value = "=sumif(indirect
($D$11),$B23,indirect($F$11))"
```

FIND A STRING OF TEXT

```
' Locate the first cell which contains the
date that is indicated, and store the cell
address in the range variable called
SearchDate.

RowNumber = ActiveSheet.Columns
(ColumnNumberToSearch).Find(What:
="TextToSearchFor", SearchOrder:=xlByRows,
SearchDirection:=xlPrevious).Row
```

FIND A DATE

If the macro needs to search for a date, the code is as follows:

```
Dim SearchDate as Range

'Find each text string on a worksheet and
replace it as indicated

Set SearchDate =
Cells.Find(What:=CDate("2/01/2020"),
After:=Range("A1"), LookIn:=xlFormulas,
LookAt:=xlWhole, SearchOrder:=xlByRows,
SearchDirection:=xlNext, MatchCase:=False)
```

FIND AND REPLACE

```
Cells.Replace What:="Old Text That Needs To
Be Replaced", Replacement:="New Text That
Needs To Replace The Old Text",
LookAt:=xlWhole, SearchOrder:=xlByRows,
MatchCase:=False, SearchFormat:=False,
ReplaceFormat:=True
```

CALCULATE THE LAST ROW AND COLUMN OF A BLOCK OF DATA

In order to specify a range of cells, it is often necessary to determine which row and/or column contains the last piece of data. This is accomplished by searching for anything, which is denoted as "*". This is combined with the "previous" search direction, and so it is important to place the cursor in cell A1 of that worksheet before typing the code which searches for anything that is found before cell A1.

```
' Place the cursor at cell A1 in order to
prepare for the search

ActiveSheet.Range("A1").Select

' Search through the specified column in a
backwards direction from the current cursor
position and provides the row number which
contains the last row of text, then stores
this row number in the numeric variable
called LastRowWithData

LastRowWithData =
ActiveSheet.Columns(ColumnNumberToSearchThro
ugh).Find(What:="*", SearchOrder:=xlByRows,
SearchDirection:=xlPrevious).Row

' Search through the specified row in a
backwards direction from the current cursor
position and provides the column number
which contains the last column of text, then
stores this column number in the numeric
variable called LastColumnWithData

LastColumnWithData =
ActiveSheet.Rows(RowNumberToSearchThrough).
Find(What:="*", SearchOrder:=xlByColumns,
SearchDirection:=xlPrevious).Column
```

These alternate methods can also be used to determine the last row or column of data:

```
'Determine the last row with data and store
it in the variable

LastRow = ActiveSheet.Cells(Rows.Count,
1).End(xlUp).Row

'Determine the last row with data and store
it in the variable

LastColumn = ActiveSheet.Cells(1,
Columns.Count).End(xlToLeft).Column
```

CONDITIONS – IF, THEN, AND, OR

An "If...Then" Statement checks for a condition to be met before running the code that follows it. At the end of this specific conditional code, there is a line which says "End If". In order to facilitate reading the code, it is common practice to indent all code within an IF statement.

When more than one condition needs to be met, the IF function can be combined with the AND function

```
If Variable1 = "Joe" And Variable2 = "Smith"
And Variable3 = "New York" Then

    Input code here

End If
```

When one of several condition must be met, the IF function can be combined with the OR function

```
If Variable1 = "Joe" Or Variable1 = "John"
Or Variable1 = "Michael" Then

    Input code here

End If
```

When one condition has several alternative options, the IF function can be combined with the ELSEIF and/or ELSE function. ELSEIF allows more than one IF statement to be applied, and only one ENDIF is used. The ELSE function provides the option to apply code for any situation that is not specified by the previous IF and ELSEIF statements. ELSE is the equivalent of instructing the macro "for all other situations that are not specified by the previous condition(s)…"

```
If Variable1 = "Joe" Then
```

   Input code here

```
ElseIf Variable1 = "John" Then
```

 Input code here

```
Else:
```

 Input code here

```
End If
```

When searching for data, search range will be "nothing" if the data is not found. IF statements can handle this situation.

```vba
Dim SearchRange as Range

Dim SearchSubString as Text

Dim ColumnToCopy as Long

' Search cell values for the string of text

Set SearchRange =
Cells.Find(What:=SearchSubString,
LookIn:=xlValues, LookAt:=xlPart,
SearchOrder:=xlByRows,
SearchDirection:=xlNext, MatchCase:=False,
SearchFormat:=False)

' If the string of text is not found, then
this variable will be equal to Nothing

    If SearchRange Is Nothing Then

' Jump to line 10 in the code

        GoTo 10

' If the above condition is not true (ie if
the string of text is found)…

    Else

' Save the column # with the text in the
ColumnToCopy numeric variable

        ColumnToCopy = SearchRange.Column

    End If
```

MEETING CRITERIA - SELECT CASE FUNCTION

Select Case is an alternative method for checking if something meets one of several possible criteria

```
Select Case ColumnHeading  'Check to see if
the current column is on the list of columns
to keep

 Case "", "ColumnName1", " ColumnName2", "
ColumnName3"  ' For these column headings...

   GoTo 110     ' Move the macro past the
following code, by jumping to line 110

 Case Else     ' For any column headings that
are not listed in the case above...

' Select the column that is determined by
the ColumnCounterNumber variable

   Columns(ColumnNumber).Select

Selection.Delete Shift:=xlToLeft ' Delete the
selected column

End Select

110 ' This is the Go To location for the
cases that are listed above. It allows the
macro to skip the code in the Case Else
section, which would have deleted the
column.
```

IGNORE ERRORS AND SUPPRESS DISPLAY ALERTS

In some cases, it is known that an error message will likely occur, however, it is also known that the error will inconsequential, and can therefore be ignored. When this is anticipated, it is possible to suppress the error message dialogue box by immediately preceding the problematic code with:

```
On Error Resume Next ' Temporarily ignore
errors, such as if there's no filter to
begin with
```

And then as soon as possible after the problematic code, the following line is needed to once again allow error messages to be communicated to the user. Although tempting, it is highly unadvisable to activate the line above without toggling off this option immediately afterwards. The consequence of not running the following line of code is that errors will not be detected at all, and this will cause the macro to be unpredictable.

```
On Error GoTo 0 ' Resume the regular error
procedure, which is to stop for any bugs in
the code.
```

Similar to the "On Error" code, there is an option to automatically select the default option for any dialogue boxes that may appear if the following code is not placed before the code which triggers the dialogue box. This is often used just before a worksheet is deleted, since Excel will display a dialogue box to verify that the user would like to delete the worksheet. Again, this feature needs to be toggled back once the problematic code has been executed.

```
Application.DisplayAlerts = False

Worksheets("Data").Delete

Application.DisplayAlerts = True
```

REPETITVE ACTIONS – FOR-NEXT LOOP

A "For... Next" loop instructs the macro to cycle a specific variable from one specified number to another, it will run a sub-routine of code, which is found between the "For" line and the "Next" line. The "Next" line instructs the macro to go back up to the "For" line. At this point the variable's value is increased by one, and the loop repeats. This repetition will continue until the variable has increased to the maximum value indicated in the range. In order to facilitate reading the code, it is common practice to indent all code within a loop.

```
Dim counter As Integer ' Declare an integer
variable called "counter" to run a loop

For counter = 0 To 10 'The looped code will
run 11 times as the variable increases from
0 to 10.

  Selection.Value = counter ' Input the value
of the counter variable into the selected
cell

  Selection.Offset(1, 0).Select ' Move the
cursor down one cell

Next counter ' Repeat the code after the
"For counter" line until the variable has
reached its maximum value
```

REPETITVE ACTIONS – FOR-EACH LOOP

A "For each cell" loop instructs the macro to cycle through all cells in a range, and for every cell, it will run a sub-routine of code, which is found between the "For each cell" line and the "Next" line. The "Next" line instructs the macro to cycle back up to the "For each" line and repeat the code for the following cell, until there are no more cells left in the range.

```
For Each Cell In
ActiveSheet.Range("A1","A99")

   If Cell.Value = 0 Then

      Cell.EntireRow.Delete

   EndIf

Next
```

The following code uses a For Each loop to un-merge cells:

```
Dim cell, joinedCells As Range

For Each cell In
ThisWorkbook.ActiveSheet.Range("A1:B4")

      If cell.MergeCells Then

            Set joinedCells = cell.MergeArea

            cell.MergeCells = False

            joinedCells.Value = cell.Value

      End If

Next
```

PIVOT TABLES

The following code can be used to set up a pivot table, step by step. A much more concise version of this method, which tends to result in fewer errors is provided below.

```
' Declare Variables

Sub InsertPivotTable()


Dim PivotWorksheet As Worksheet

Dim DataWorksheet As Worksheet

Dim PivotCache1 As PivotCache

Dim PivotTable1 As PivotTable

Dim PivotDataRange As Range

Dim LastRow As Long

Dim LastCol As Long
```

```vba
' Alternative 1: Insert the pivot table into
an existing worksheet

Set PivotWorksheet =
Worksheets("PivotTable")

Set DataWorksheet = Worksheets("Data")

Worksheets("PivotTable").Activate

On Error Resume Next

ActiveSheet.PivotTables("PivotTable1").Table
Range2.Clear


'Alternative 2: Insert the pivot table into
a new blank worksheet

On Error Resume Next

Application.DisplayAlerts = False

Worksheets("PivotTable").Delete

Sheets.Add Before:=ActiveSheet

ActiveSheet.Name = "PivotTable"

Application.DisplayAlerts = True

Set PivotWorksheet =
Worksheets("PivotTable")

Set DataWorksheet = Worksheets("Data")
```

```vba
' Define Data Range

LastRow = ActiveSheet.Cells(Rows.Count,
1).End(xlUp).Row

LastCol = ActiveSheet.Cells(1,
Columns.Count).End(xlToLeft).Column

Set PivotDataRange = ActiveSheet.Cells(1,
1).Resize(LastRow, LastCol)


' Define Pivot Cache

Set PivotCache1 =
ActiveWorkbook.PivotCaches.Create(SourceType
:=xlDatabase,
SourceData:=PivotDataRange).CreatePivotTable
(TableDestination:=PivotWorksheet.Cells(2,
2), TableName:="PivotTable1")


' Insert Blank Pivot Table

Set PivotTable1 =
PivotCache1.CreatePivotTable
(TableDestination:=PivotWorksheet.Cells(1,
1), TableName:="PivotTable1")
```

The following is an alternative method to create a pivot table with more concise code, which is often preferable:

```
' Create a pivot table on cell A3 of the
"PivotTableWorksheet", which has its source
data in the "Data" worksheet from A2:J99

ActiveWorkbook.PivotCaches.Create(SourceType
:=xlDatabase, SourceData:="Data!R2C1:R99C10"
, Version:=xlPivotTableVersion12)
.CreatePivotTable TableDestination:=
"PivotTableWorksheet!R3C1",
TableName:="PivotTable1", DefaultVersion:=
xlPivotTableVersion12
```

PIVOT TABLE FIELDS SETUP

'The Currency field is set up to appear as rows in the pivot table

```
' Insert Row Fields

With ActiveSheet.PivotTables("PivotTable1").
PivotFields("Year")

    .Orientation = xlRowField

    .Position = 1

End With

With ActiveSheet.PivotTables("PivotTable1").
PivotFields("Month")

    .Orientation = xlRowField

    .Position = 2

End With

' The Currency field is set up as a column

With ActiveSheet.PivotTables("PivotTable1").
PivotFields("Currency")

    .Orientation = xlColumnField

    .Position = 1

End With
```

```vba
' Insert Value aka Data Field

With ActiveSheet.PivotTables("PivotTable1")
    .PivotFields ("Amount")
    .Orientation = xlDataField
    .Function = xlSum
    .NumberFormat = "#,##0"
    .Name = "Revenue "

End With

ActiveSheet.PivotTables("PivotTable1").AddDa
taField

' The AccountCode is set up as a count value
field in the pivot table

ActiveSheet.PivotTables("PivotTable1").Pivot
Fields("AccountCode "), "Count of
AccountCode ", xlCount

' The Fee value field is changed to be a sum
value in the pivot table

With ActiveSheet.PivotTables("PivotTable1").
PivotFields("Count of Fee")

        .Caption = "Sum of Fee"

        .Function = xlSum

    End With

    ' Set up a formula within the pivot which
subtracts January from February

ActiveSheet.PivotTables("PivotTable1").Pivot
Fields("Month").CalculatedItems. Add
"Formula1", "='February' -'January'", True
```

PIVOT TABLE FILTERS

```
'The payment column is set up as a filter

With

ActiveSheet.PivotTables("PivotTable1").Pivot
Fields("Payment")

    .Orientation = xlPageField

    .Position = 1

End With



' Filtered values are indicated for the
Payment field

    With

ActiveSheet.PivotTables("PivotTable1").Pivot
Fields("Payment")

    .PivotItems("Subtotal").Visible = True

    .PivotItems("Local Tax").Visible = False

.PivotItems("Federal Tax ").Visible = False

End With
```

The following alternative method can be used to set up the filters within a pivot table

```
' Filtered values are indicated for the
Month field.

ActiveSheet.PivotTables(PivotTableName).Pivo
tFields("Month").ClearAllFilters

    On Error Resume Next

    With

ActiveSheet.PivotTables(PivotTableName).Pivo
tFields("Month")


PivotSheet.PivotTables(PivotTableName).Allow
MultipleFilters = True

'The filter will make this field invisible

    .PivotItems("January").Visible = False

'The filter will make this field visible
    .PivotItems("February ").Visible = True

'The filter will make this field invisible

    .PivotItems("March ").Visible = True

    End With


'Sort the division field in descending order
based on the by count of the discrepancies

ActiveSheet.PivotTables("PivotTable1").Pivot
Fields("Division").AutoSort xlDescending,
"Count of Discrepancy"
```

```vba
' This sub-routine removes all subtotals
from the pivot table using a more compact
and universal method than the regular macro
record method, which lists all values for
all variables.

    Dim PivTbl As PivotTable

    Dim PivFld As PivotField

    On Error Resume Next

    For Each PivTbl In
Application.ActiveSheet.PivotTables

        For Each PivFld In PivTbl.PivotFields

        PivFld.Subtotals(1) = True

        PivFld.Subtotals(1) = False

    Next

    Next

    On Error GoTo 0



' Remove grand totals from rows and columns

    With ActiveSheet.PivotTables("PivotTable1")

        .ColumnGrand = False

        .RowGrand = False

    End With
```

```vba
' Determine the last row in the pivot table
    With
ActiveSheet.PivotTables("PivotTable1").Table
Range1

        Lastrow =
ActiveSheet.UsedRange.Rows.Count

    End With
```

```vba
' Format Pivot Table

ActiveSheet.PivotTables("PivotTable1").ShowT
ableStyleRowStripes = True

ActiveSheet.PivotTables("PivotTable1").Table
Style2 = "PivotStyleMedium9"

End Sub
```

```vba
' Change pivot design to "Compact"

ActiveSheet.PivotTables("PivotTable1").RowAx
isLayout xlCompactRow

' Change pivot design to "Tabular"

ActiveSheet.PivotTables("PivotTable1").RowAx
isLayout xlTabularRow
```

DISPLAY A MESSAGE TO THE USER

```vba
MsgBox "Input Your Message Here"   ' This
```
code makes a dialogue box appear with a
message and an OK button that closes the
dialogue box.

SPEED UP A SLOW MACRO

Sometimes a macro is operating too slowly when handling large amounts of data. One way to speed it up is to input code just before the problematic code, which temporarily disables automatic calculations and the updates to the computer screen, which often appears to flicker unintelligibly when macros are being executed. After the problematic code, this is then toggled back to its regular settings.

```
' Turn off the automatic calculations and
screen updates, to speed up the macro.

    Application.Calculation = xlManual

    Application.ScreenUpdating = True

    Application.DisplayStatusBar = False

    Application.EnableEvents = False

' Turn on the automatic calculations and
screen updates, which were deactivated so as
not to slow down the macro.

    Application.Calculation = xlAutomatic

    Application.ScreenUpdating = True

    Application.DisplayStatusBar = True

    Application.EnableEvents = True
```

RUN A DIFFERENT MACRO, THEN CONTINUE WITH THE CURRENT MACRO

If some code is used many times within a macro, or if it is used in different macros, it is possible to set up a separate macro for that code, and then it can be called upon when needed.

```
' Set up a separate sub for this sub-
routine, then in the main sub, just type the
sub (macro) name on its own.

Public Sub WaitABit()

' Wait a few seconds

    Application.Wait (Now +
TimeValue("00:00:02"))

End Sub



'In the main sub, this code will run the
subroutine

    WaitABit
```

UPDATE A WORKSHEET IN A DIFFERENT FILE

Since macros can be difficult to maintain and understand within a group of people, it is often helpful to keep a macro in a separate file from the files that are circulated among colleagues.

```vba
Sub UpdateWorksheetFromDifferentFile()

    Dim MyFileName, FileFolder As String ' Establish
the variables to store strings of text

    Dim WorksheetNumber As Integer ' Establish a
variable's name and sets it up to store an
integer which can be very large if needed

    FileFolder = "c:\testfolder\" ' Set up the variable
to hold the folder path with the files

    MyFileName = "Book1.xlsx" ' Set up this
variable to hold the file called Book1.xlsx

    Workbooks.Open (FileFolder & MyFileName) ' Open
the spreadsheet file that is defined by the
FileFolder and MyFileName variables

    Worksheets("Sheet1").Activate ' Activate the
worksheet called "Sheet1"

    Range("A1") = "12/16/2024" ' Input Dec 16, 2024
into cell A1 in that worksheet

    ActiveWorkbook.Save ' Save the spreadsheet
that is currently active

    ActiveWorkbook.Close ' Close the spreadsheet
that is currently active

End Sub
```

UPDATE MULTIPLE WORKSHEETS FROM MULTIPLE FILES

The following code will cycle through all of the files that are in a folder, and apply code to each one. It is important to only place the relevant files in the folder when using this code.

```
Sub UpdateWorksheetsFromDifferentFiles()

    Dim MyFileName As String ' Establish a variable
and sets it up to store a string of text

    Dim FileFolder As String ' Establish a variable
and sets it up to store a string of text

    Dim WorksheetNumber As Long ' Set a variable
to store a number which can be very large

    FileFolder = "c:\testfolder\" ' Set up the variable
to hold the folder path with the files

MyFileName = Dir(FileFolder) ' Set up the filename
variable

Do While Len(MyFileName) > 0 ' Begin a loop that
continues for all files

    If MyFileName = "Book9.xlsm" Then ' This sets up
an IF condition that affects the file which
contains the macro code.

        Exit Sub ' The code stops for the file
specified by this condition.

    End If ' This ends the code which applies to
the IF condition.

    Workbooks.open(FileFolder & MyFileName) ' Open the
file
```

For <u>WorksheetNumber</u>=1 to **application.worksheets. count** ' Count the number of worksheets and sets the number as the upper range in this For-Next loop

Worksheets(<u>WorksheetNumber</u>).Activate ' Go into the Worksheet number that the For-Next loop is currently on

Range("**A1**") = "**12/16/2024**" ' Input Dec 16, 2024 into cell A1 of the active worksheet

Next WorksheetNumber ' Send the program back up to the "For" line and increas the counter by one

ActiveWorkBook.Save ' Save the active spreadsheet file

ActiveWorkBook.close ' Close the active spreadsheet file

<u>MyFileName</u> = Dir(<u>FileFolder</u>) ' Set up the filename variable

Loop ' Send the program back up to the "Do While" line, so that it repeats as long as the "Do While" condition is applicable

End Sub

CONTROLLING THE KEYBOARD USING A MACRO

This section explains how to use a macro to send commands to the keyboard, so that the computer can access programs outside of Excel. Any macro can cause unintended negative consequences when used improperly, however this is even more of a risk when the macro is used to automatically control the keyboard. It is crucial to note that this code sends commands to the keyboard extremely quickly, and so unanticipated delays in execution can have serious consequences when applying this code.

It cannot be stressed enough that this approach should be used as rarely as possible, and in a manner which will not cause unintended consequences, such as accidentally deleting files or typing passwords into the wrong fields. If the Excel window is not activated, the CTRL-BREAK or CTRL-PAUSE feature will not work, and so it will be very difficult to stop the macro in the event of an error, such as an unexpected dialogue box, error message, pop-up, etc. In these situations it may be necessary to stop the macro by pressing CTRL-ALT-DELETE and shutting down Excel completely.

The appropriate key codes are placed between the quotation marks of the following code:

```
Application.SendKeys (" ")
```

For example, it may be necessary to press backspace, then press tab three times, then type Michael, then press enter

```
Application.SendKeys ("{BACKSPACE}")

Application.SendKeys ("{TAB}{TAB}{TAB}")

Application.SendKeys ("Michael")

Application.SendKeys ("{ENTER}")
```

Other Keyboard Codes:

BACKSPACE {BACKSPACE} or {BS} or {BKSP}
BREAK {BREAK}
CAPS LOCK {CAPSLOCK}
PRINT SCREEN {PRTSC}
SCROLL LOCK {SCROLLLOCK}
INS or INSERT {INSERT} {INS}
DEL or DELETE {DELETE} or {DEL}
ENTER {ENTER} or ~
ESC {ESC}
HELP {HELP}

HOME {HOME}
END {END}
UP ARROW {UP}
DOWN ARROW {DOWN}
RIGHT ARROW {RIGHT}
LEFT ARROW {LEFT}
NUM LOCK {NUMLOCK}
PAGE DOWN {PGDN}
PAGE UP {PGUP}
TAB {TAB}

F1 {F1}	F5 {F5}	F9 {F9}	F13 {F13}
F2 {F2}	F6 {F6}	F10 {F10}	F14 {F14}
F3 {F3}	F7 {F7}	F11 {F11}	F15 {F15}
F4 {F4}	F8 {F8}	F12 {F12}	F16 {F16}

To specify keys combined with any combination of the SHIFT, CTRL, and ALT keys, precede the key code with one or more of the following key codes:

SHIFT: +
CTRL: ^
ALT: %

To specify that any combination of SHIFT, CTRL, and ALT should be held down while several other keys are pressed, enclose the code for those keys in parentheses. For example, to specify to hold down SHIFT while E and C are pressed, use "

=+(EC)

To specify to hold down SHIFT while E is pressed, followed by C without SHIFT, use

=+EC

OPENING MULTIPLE FILES THAT ARE NOT EXCEL SPREADSHEETS

Sometimes it is necessary to search for data in several files that are not spreadsheets, and input specific data into Excel, This code loops through all of the files in a folder, which are PDF's in this case

```
' Set up the filename variable
FileName = Dir(FileFolder & "*")

Do While Len(FileName) > 0 ' Begin a loop
that continues for all files

' Open the file
   Shell AdobePdfReader & " " & FileFolder &
FileName, vbMaximizedFocus

Application.SendKeys ("^a^c") ' Press CTRL-A
to select all and CTRL-C to copy

' Press ALT-F4 to close Adobe
Application.SendKeys ("%{F4}")

AppActivate Title:=ThisWorkbook.Application.
Caption ' Activate Excel

' Activate the worksheet
Workbooks("spreadsheet.xlsm").Worksheets("Sh
eet1").Activate

   LastRowToCopy = ActiveSheet.Columns(1).
Find(What:="*", SearchOrder:=xlByRows,
SearchDirection:=xlPrevious).Row 'Find the
last non-blank cell in the column to copy

' Go one cell below the last cell with data
in column A
Workbooks("spreadsheet.xlsm").Worksheets("Sh
eet1").Cells(LastRowToCopy + 1, 1).Select

   ActiveSheet.Paste
```

```vb
   ' Set up the next filename variable
   FileName = Dir

Loop ' Send the program back up to the "Do
While" line to repeat the code
```

HOW TO PERFORM OTHER FUNCTIONS:

Macro Record

Microsoft Office has a "Macro Record" feature in each of its main programs which allows the user to record a series of steps within that program. If this feature is used, then the basic code will be automatically prepared which allows the user to repeat exactly what was done during the recording. To get the most out of this feature, it is recommended that the user applies the methods explained above to modify the code that was automatically prepared by the recording processes. This will make the Macro Record feature significantly more dynamic, flexible, and useful.

Blogs

Although it may be difficult to believe, there are countless blogs online where people have asked how to perform a specific task using a macro, and the experts actually share their best code. So at the risk of appearing lazy, the best solution for figuring out how to write a macro is to Google it! When performing this type of Google search query using a search engine, it is often best to input "excel vba macro" before the function that you need to use, such as:

```
excel vba macro align all text
```

The websites called mrexcel and stackoverflow are by far the most helpful, with code that is as simple and generic as possible. The code in these websites is presented in special text boxes that are easily copied, and almost all of the code has been verified by the requester as well as other users. There is even feedback from those who have requested help, and suggestions for improvement from other experts.

Youtube

A third method that can be particularly helpful for learning to write macros is to search for Youtube videos. There are hundreds, if not thousands of excellent videos with detailed walkthroughs on any topic.

MAKE A BUTTON ON THE SPREADSHEET TO ACTIVATE A MACRO

Click Developer in the Menu Bar (aka in the "Ribbon")

Click: Insert > Button

Click: Assign Macro

Select a Macro that has already been coded

Draw the button onto the spreadsheet

Type a caption inside the button to label it.

PRACTICE:

We can use a macro to generate some raw data, which we can then use to practice writing macros. In this scenario, imagine that this data will be provided every month, with the potential for this frequency to increase in the future to a weekly or even daily basis. It will be necessary to use a macro to automate all of the following steps so that this work can be done in a few minutes instead of a few hours. It is always a good idea to keep a copy of the raw data in its original format. Append all new code after the exiting code as you move forward through the drafts.

Assignment: The 1st Draft

1) Run the raw data generator macro, which is provided before the solution.

2) Make a copy of the entire raw data tab.

3) Rename the new tab so that it is called "Clean Data".

4) Place the summation formula at the end of the first row, which adds up all of the previous columns except for the first column.

5) Copy and paste the formula to all of the rows below, up to the last row, and label this column heading "Total".

6) Input an auto-filter into the top row.

7) Set up a For-Next loop which removes the "ID " characters from all of the rows in the first column, because those non-numeric values would limit our ability to work with those row labels.

8) Set up a For-Next loop to check each column for a row that contains a non-numeric value or a blank cell. Then remove the entire row that contains either of these conditions.

9) Use a For-Next loop within a For-Next loop to divide all of the numbers from the 2nd to the 2nd last column by 100, because the data is in cents instead of dollars.

10) For the columns that contain Friday amounts it will be necessary to divide each of those amounts by 2. Friday columns are days 5, 10, 15, and 20. This is because of an unavoidable system error whereby the data includes both the debit and also the credit transactions, which are therefore duplicated in the raw data for those days. Use the nested For-Next loop

11) The data now needs to then be displayed in groupings. Set up a For-Next loop which performs the following code 10 times. Filter the clean data tab so that the first column shows ID values that are to be greater than 0 and duplicate this filtered tab, placing the new tab at the end of all tabs. Rename the newly duplicated tab so that it is called "ID > 0". In the next loop, filter the clean data tab to display ID numbers 100 or greater, then duplicate the filtered tab and place the new tab at the end of all tabs. Rename the newly duplicated tab so that it is called "ID > 100". Repeat for ID numbers > 300, 400, etc.

Assignment: The 2nd Draft

The filters ended up having too much information, and so we need to change each of the tabs so that they only contain tranches of 100 ID numbers in each tab. Filter each tab and delete any rows with ID numbers that are outside of the bracket of 100 per tab. This way, each tab will only contain 100 ID numbers at a time, and this will eliminate a lot of confusion. For example one tab should only contain rows with ID numbers 101 to 200. This can be done for all worksheets.

Assignment: The 3rd Draft

1) Update column A by inserting "ID "into each row, before the ID number. In order to help with sorting, for ID numbers that are less than 10, insert 3 zeros before the number. For ID numbers 10-99, insert 2 zeros, and insert 1 zero for 100-999.

2) In the "Clean Data" tab, un-filter the data to display all rows.

3) Insert a new blank worksheet after all of the worksheets.

4) Rename this last worksheet so that it is called "Pivot".

5) Place the cursor in the "Clean Data" tab in cell A1.

6) Program the macro so that it calculates the last row with data.

7) Use this number to set up a pivot table in the "Pivot" tab, with the source data being the "Clean Data" tab.

8) Insert rows into the pivot table for customer ID, then set up a For-Next loop for all the columns. Every day should be inserted as a column in the pivot table.

9) Remove all subtotals from the pivot table.

10) Change the pivot table into the tabular format.

11) Set up the pivot table so that it has grand totals for the rows but not for the columns.

12) Remove the stripes from the design of the pivot table and use the style called "pivot style medium 9".

13) Delete all worksheets starting from the second-last tab to tab number five. This needs to be done with a For-Next loop that counts down instead of counting up. Do this by inserting Step -1 at the end of the code in the "For" line.

14) Program the macro so that it calculates the last row in the pivot table.

15) Insert a new blank worksheet before all of the other tabs, and rename it so that it is called "Summary".

16) Copy all of the Pivot Table cells and paste values into the summary tab.

Assignment: The 4th Draft

1) Unfilter all of the cells in the "Clean Data" tab.

2) Duplicate this tab, and place this copy so that it appears at the end of all of the tabs.

3) Rename the last tab so that it is called "Rearranged".

4) Program the macro so that it calculates the last row with data.

5) Use a For-Next loop to select all of the cells one column at a time, beginning at column B. Exclude the headings.

6) Copy this column of values, and paste it as values below the last row, in column C. Exclude the headings.

7) Copy column A, and paste it as values below the last row, in column A. Be sure not to repeat the headings.

8) For column B, input "Day 2".

9) After the For-Next loop has moved all of the days down into a long format, delete rows 2 to 770. Also delete columns D to V.

10) This will vastly improve the appearance of the pivot table and make it more dynamic, since it will not have 20 different columns of data but rather it will have all the daily amounts treated as values, which can be used in a more functional and dynamic and workable. Delete the Pivot tab, and repeat steps 3 to 12 from the instructions for the 3rd Draft above.

11) Delete the "Summary" tab. Then repeat steps 14 to 16 from the instructions for the 3rd Draft above.

If this macro was programmed correctly, day 15 for CustID 900 will be equal to 43.11 on the pivot tab.

DATA GENERATOR MACRO:

```
Sub CreateData()              ' Automatic data
generator

Dim RowCounter As Long

Dim ColumnCounter As Long

For ColumnCounter = 1 To 21

    For RowCounter = 1 To 1001

        Cells(RowCounter,
ColumnCounter).Value = Round(RowCounter ^ (3
/ 4) + (RowCounter * 4.3 + ColumnCounter) +
ColumnCounter ^ 2, 0) ' Use this calculation
to populate all of the values

        If ColumnCounter > 1 And
Round((Cells(RowCounter,
ColumnCounter).Value) / 36, 0) =
((Cells(RowCounter, ColumnCounter).Value) /
36) Then Cells(RowCounter,
ColumnCounter).Value = "" ' If the cell
value is divisible by 36, make the cell
blank

        If (Cells(RowCounter,
ColumnCounter).Value >= 65 And
Cells(RowCounter, ColumnCounter).Value <=
90) Or (Cells(RowCounter,
ColumnCounter).Value >= 97 And
Cells(RowCounter, ColumnCounter).Value <=
122) Then Cells(RowCounter,
ColumnCounter).Value = Chr(Cells(RowCounter,
ColumnCounter).Value) & Cells(RowCounter,
ColumnCounter).Value ' If the cell contains
a value within these ranges,  derive the
ASCII character for that value, and place
the character before the value. When these
ranges are placed into the CHR function,
this will result in the alphabet.
```

```vba
    ' Insert ID numbers into column A. Use
zeros before the numbers so that all rows
have a 4 digit ID number.

    If RowCounter < 10 + 1 Then

        If ColumnCounter = 1 Then
Cells(RowCounter, 1).Value = "ID 000" &
RowCounter - 1

        ElseIf RowCounter >= 10 + 1 And
RowCounter < 101 Then

        If ColumnCounter = 1 Then
Cells(RowCounter, 1).Value = "ID 00" &
RowCounter - 1

        ElseIf RowCounter >= 99 + 1 And
RowCounter < 1001 Then

        If ColumnCounter = 1 Then
Cells(RowCounter, 1).Value = "ID 0" &
RowCounter - 1

        ElseIf RowCounter >= 1000 + 1 And
RowCounter < 10000 Then

        If ColumnCounter = 1 Then
Cells(RowCounter, 1).Value = "ID " &
RowCounter - 1

    End If

    ' Label the first row with "Day "
followed by the day number.

        If RowCounter = 1 And ColumnCounter
<= 10 Then Cells(1, ColumnCounter).Value =
"Day 0" & ColumnCounter - 1

        If RowCounter = 1 And ColumnCounter
> 10 Then Cells(1, ColumnCounter).Value =
"Day " & ColumnCounter - 1
```

```
        Cells(RowCounter,
ColumnCounter).HorizontalAlignment = xlRight

    Next RowCounter

Next ColumnCounter

Cells(1, 1).Value = "CustID"

End Sub
```

SOLUTION:

```vba
Sub DataProcessingMacro()


' DRAFT 1:

' DRAFT 1: Step 1 is provided separate from
this solution in the previous text.


' DRAFT 1: Step 2

' Rename the active tab
ActiveSheet.Name = "Raw Data"

ActiveSheet.Copy After:=Sheets(1) ' Duplicat
the tab, places the copy after the 1st tab


' DRAFT 1: Step 3

' Rename the active tab

Sheets(2).Name = "Clean Data"

Sheets("Clean Data").Activate


' DRAFT 1: Step 4

Range("V2").FormulaR1C1 = "=SUM(RC[-21]:RC[-
1])"  ' Add the amounts from cells B2 to U2
(ie 21 to 1 columns to the left)
```

```vba
' DRAFT 1: Step 5

Range("V2").Select

Selection.Copy

Range("V3:V1001").Select

ActiveSheet.Paste

Application.CutCopyMode = False ' Remove
clipboard cut/copy border (aka "ants")

Range("V1").Value = "Total"


' DRAFT 1: Step 6

Range("A1:V1").Select

' Place an autofilter on the cell selection,
or remove the autofilter if there already is
one
```

```vba
Selection.AutoFilter

' DRAFT 1: Step 7

For ColumnCounter = 1 To 21


    For RowCounter = 2 To 1001


        If ColumnCounter = 1 Then
Cells(RowCounter, 1).Value =
WorksheetFunction.Substitute(Cells(RowCounte
r, 1).Value, "ID ", "") ' Substitute "ID "
with nothing


        ' DRAFT 1: Step 9

        If ColumnCounter <> 1 And
WorksheetFunction.IsNumber(Cells(RowCounter,
ColumnCounter).Value) = True Then
Cells(RowCounter, ColumnCounter).Value =
Round(Cells(RowCounter, ColumnCounter).Value
/ 100, 2) ' Divide all numeric values by 100
```

```
' DRAFT 1: Step 10

' If the column number is divisible by 5,
divide the cell value by 2

        If ColumnCounter <> 1 And
WorksheetFunction.IsNumber(Cells(RowCounter,
ColumnCounter).Value) = True And
ColumnCounter / 5 = Round(ColumnCounter / 5,
0) Then Cells(RowCounter,
ColumnCounter).Value =
Round(Cells(RowCounter, ColumnCounter).Value
/ 2, 2)


    Next RowCounter
```

```
' DRAFT 1: Step 8

' Temporarily ignore errors, such as if
there's no filter to begin with

    On Error Resume Next

        Range(Cells(2, ColumnCounter),
Cells(1001,
ColumnCounter)).SpecialCells(xlCellTypeBlank
s).EntireRow.Delete 'Delete all blank rows

'Delete all non-numeric rows

        Range(Cells(2, ColumnCounter),
Cells(1001,
ColumnCounter)).SpecialCells(xlCellTypeConst
ants, 2).EntireRow.Delete

    On Error GoTo 0 ' Resume the regular
error procedure which is to stop for any
bugs in the code


Next ColumnCounter
```

```vba
' DRAFT 1: Step 11

Dim TabCounter As Integer

For TabCounter = 1 To 10

    Sheets("Clean Data").Activate

' Temporarily ignore errors, such as if
there's no filter to begin with

    On Error Resume Next

        ActiveSheet.ShowAllData        '
Unfilter any filtered data

' Resume the regular error procedure which
is to stop for any bugs in the code

    On Error GoTo 0

ActiveSheet.Range("$A$1:$V$1001").AutoFilter
Field:=1, Criteria1:=">" & (TabCounter * 100
+ 1), Operator:=xlAnd

' Duplicate the tab, and plac the copy after
the last tab

    ActiveSheet.Copy
After:=Sheets(Sheets.Count)

    Sheets(Sheets.Count).Name = "ID=<" &
TabCounter * 100 ' Rename the active tab

Next TabCounter
```

```vba
'DRAFT 2

Dim Brackets As String

For TabCounter = 1 To 10

    Sheets("ID=<" & TabCounter *
100).Activate

' Temporarily ignore errors, such as if
there's no filter

    On Error Resume Next

        ActiveSheet.ShowAllData        '
Unfilter any filtered data

' Resume the regular error procedure which
is to stop for any bugs

    On Error GoTo 0

    Brackets = ">" & (TabCounter * 100)


ActiveSheet.Range("$A$1:$V$1001").AutoFilter
Field:=1, Criteria1:=Brackets

' Select only the visible cells which are
not filtered.

    If TabCounter <> 10 Then
Range("A2:V1001").SpecialCells(xlCellTypeVis
ible).Select

    If TabCounter <> 10 Then
Selection.EntireRow.Delete

' Temporarily ignore errors, such as if
there's no filter

    On Error Resume Next
```

```vba
        ActiveSheet.ShowAllData        '
Unfilter any filtered data

' Resume the regular error procedure which
is to stop for any bugs

    On Error GoTo 0

Next TabCounter


'DRAFT 3

' DRAFT 3: Step 1

For RowCounter = 2 To 1001

    If Cells(RowCounter, 1).Value < 10 Then
Cells(RowCounter, 1).Value = "ID 000" &
Cells(RowCounter, 1).Value

    If Cells(RowCounter, 1).Value >= 10 And
Cells(RowCounter, 1).Value < 100 Then
Cells(RowCounter, 1).Value = "ID 00" &
Cells(RowCounter, 1).Value

    If Cells(RowCounter, 1).Value >= 100 And
Cells(RowCounter, 1).Value < 1000 Then
Cells(RowCounter, 1).Value = "ID 0" &
Cells(RowCounter, 1).Value

    If Cells(RowCounter, 1).Value >= 1000
And Cells(RowCounter, 1).Value < 10000 Then
Cells(RowCounter, 1).Value = "ID " &
Cells(RowCounter, 1).Value

Next RowCounter
```

```vba
For ColumnCounter = 2 To 21

    Cells(1, ColumnCounter).Value =
ColumnCounter - 1

Next ColumnCounter

Dim LastRowWithData As Long


' DRAFT 3: Step 2

' Temporarily ignore errors, such as if
there's no filter to begin with

On Error Resume Next

    Sheets("Clean Data").ShowAllData       '
Unfilter any filtered data

' Resume the regular error procedure which
is to stop for any bugs


On Error GoTo 0

' DRAFT 3: Step 3

' Insert a blank tab after the last tab


Sheets.Add After:=Sheets(Sheets.Count)

' DRAFT 3: Step 4

' Rename the active tab"
```

```vba
Sheets(Sheets.Count).Name = "Pivot"

' DRAFT 3: Step 5

Sheets("Pivot").Activate

Range("A1").Select ' Place the cursor at
cell A1 in order to prepare for the search



' DRAFT 3: Step 6

LastRowWithData = Sheets("Clean
Data").Columns(1).Find(What:="*",
SearchOrder:=xlByRows,
SearchDirection:=xlPrevious).Row ' Search
through the specified column in a backwards
direction from the current cursor position
and provides the row number which contains
the last row of text, then stores this row
number in the numeric variable called
LastRowWithData



' DRAFT 3: Step 7

' Create a pivot table on cell A3 of the
"Pivot" tab, which has its source data in
the "Clean Data" worksheet
```

```vba
ActiveWorkbook.PivotCaches.Create(SourceType
:=xlDatabase, SourceData:="Clean
Data!R1C1:R" & LastRowWithData & "C21",
Version:=xlPivotTableVersion12).CreatePivotT
able TableDestination:="Pivot!R3C1",
TableName:="PivotTable1",
DefaultVersion:=xlPivotTableVersion12

' DRAFT 3: Step 8

' Insert Row Fields

With
ActiveSheet.PivotTables("PivotTable1").Pivot
Fields("CustID")

    .Orientation = xlRowField

    .Position = 1

End With

For ColumnCounter = 1 To 20

    ' Insert Value Fields


ActiveSheet.PivotTables("PivotTable1").AddDa
taField
ActiveSheet.PivotTables("PivotTable1").Pivot
Fields(ColumnCounter), "Sum of " &
ColumnCounter, xlSum

Next ColumnCounter
```

```vba
' DRAFT 3: Step 9

' This sub-routine removes all subtotals
from the pivot table using a more compact
and universal method than the regular macro
record method, which lists all values for
all variables.

Dim PivTbl As PivotTable

Dim PivFld As PivotField

On Error Resume Next

    For Each PivTbl In
Application.ActiveSheet.PivotTables

        For Each PivFld In
PivTbl.PivotFields

            PivFld.Subtotals(1) = True

            PivFld.Subtotals(1) = False

        Next

    Next

On Error GoTo 0



' DRAFT 3: Step 10

ActiveSheet.PivotTables("PivotTable1").RowAx
isLayout xlTabularRow       ' Change pivot
design to "Tabular"
```

```vba
' DRAFT 3: Step 11

' Remove grand totals from columns but keep
them for rows

With ActiveSheet.PivotTables("PivotTable1")

    .ColumnGrand = False

    .RowGrand = True

End With


' DRAFT 3: Step 12

' Format Pivot Table

ActiveSheet.PivotTables("PivotTable1").ShowTableStyleRowStripes = False

ActiveSheet.PivotTables("PivotTable1").TableStyle2 = "PivotStyleMedium9"
```

```vba
' DRAFT 3: Step 13

Application.DisplayAlerts = False '
Select the default option on dialogue box to
confirm worksheet deletion

For TabCounter =
(ActiveWorkbook.Sheets.Count - 1) To 5 Step
-1

    Sheets(TabCounter).Delete ' Delete the
worksheet tab

Next TabCounter

Application.DisplayAlerts = True '      Reset
the default option on dialogue box that
confirms worksheet deletion


' DRAFT 3: Step 14

Dim LastRowPivot As Long

Dim LastColumnPivot As Long

'Determine the last row in the pivot table

With
ActiveSheet.PivotTables("PivotTable1").Table
Range1

    LastRowPivot =
Sheets("Pivot").UsedRange.Rows.Count

    LastColumnPivot =
Sheets("Pivot").UsedRange.Columns.Count

End With
```

```vba
' DRAFT 3: Step 15

Sheets.Add Before:=Sheets(1) ' Insert a
blank tab before the last tab

Sheets(1).Name = "Summary" ' Rename the
active tab"


' DRAFT 3: Step 16

Sheets("Summary").Activate

Range("A1").Activate

Sheets("Pivot").Activate

Range(Cells(1, 1), Cells(LastRowPivot,
LastColumnPivot)).Select

Selection.Copy

Sheets("Summary").Activate

Selection.PasteSpecial Paste:=xlPasteValues,
Operation:=xlNone, SkipBlanks:=False,
Transpose:=False 'Paste Values

Application.CutCopyMode = False ' Remove
clipboard cut/copy border (aka "ants")

'DRAFT 4

' DRAFT 4: Step 1

Sheets("Clean Data").Activate
```

```vba
' DRAFT 4: Step 2

ActiveSheet.Copy After:=Sheets(Sheets.Count)
' Duplicate the tab, and place the copy
after the 1nd tab


' DRAFT 4: Step 3

Sheets(Sheets.Count).Name = "Rearranged" '
Rename the active tab"


' DRAFT 4: Step 4

Sheets("Rearranged").Activate

' Place the cursor at cell A1 in order to
prepare for the search

Range("A1").Select

LastRowWithData =
ActiveSheet.Columns(1).Find(What:="*",
SearchOrder:=xlByRows,
SearchDirection:=xlPrevious).Row ' Search
through the specified column in a backwards
direction from the current cursor position
and provides the row number which contains
the last row of text, then stores this row
number in the numeric variable called
LastRowWithData
```

```
' DRAFT 4: Step 5

For ColumnCounter = 1 To 20

    'Copy the values for the current day's
column

    Range(Cells(2, ColumnCounter + 1),
Cells(LastRowWithData, ColumnCounter +
1)).Select   ' Select the values in column B

    Selection.Copy


    ' DRAFT 4: Step 6

    If ColumnCounter = 1 Then
Cells((LastRowWithData * ColumnCounter) + 1,
3).Select

    If ColumnCounter > 1 Then
Cells(((LastRowWithData - 1) *
ColumnCounter) + 2, 3).Select

    Selection.PasteSpecial
Paste:=xlPasteValues, Operation:=xlNone,
SkipBlanks:=False, Transpose:=False 'Paste
Values
```

```vba
' DRAFT 4: Step 7

'Copy the row labels for the current day

    Range(Cells(2, 1),
Cells(LastRowWithData, 1)).Select

    Selection.Copy

    If ColumnCounter = 1 Then
Cells((LastRowWithData * ColumnCounter) + 1,
1).Select

    If ColumnCounter > 1 Then
Cells(((LastRowWithData - 1) *
ColumnCounter) + 2, 1).Select

    Selection.PasteSpecial
Paste:=xlPasteValues, Operation:=xlNone,
SkipBlanks:=False, Transpose:=False 'Paste
Values
```

```vba
' DRAFT 4: Step 8

'Copy the column label for the current
day

Cells(1, ColumnCounter + 1).Select

Selection.Copy

If ColumnCounter = 1 Then
Range(Cells(LastRowWithData * ColumnCounter
+ 1, 2), Cells(LastRowWithData *
(ColumnCounter + 1) - 1, 2)).Select

If ColumnCounter > 1 Then
Range(Cells((LastRowWithData - 1) *
ColumnCounter + 2, 2),
Cells((LastRowWithData - 1) * (ColumnCounter
+ 1) + 1, 2)).Select

'Paste Values

    Selection.PasteSpecial
Paste:=xlPasteValues, Operation:=xlNone,
SkipBlanks:=False, Transpose:=False

Next ColumnCounter
```

```vba
' DRAFT 4: Step 9

' Delete the old table

Rows("2:770").Delete

Columns("D:V").Delete ' Delete the old table

' Label column B

Range("B1").Value = "Day"

Range("C1").Value = "Amount ($)" ' Label
column B
```

```vba
' DRAFT 4: Step 10

' Temporarily ignore errors, such as if
there's no filter

On Error Resume Next

    Sheets("Clean Data").ShowAllData        '
Unfilter any filtered data

' Resume the regular error procedure which
is to stop for any bugs

On Error GoTo 0

Application.DisplayAlerts = False '
Select the default option on dialogue box to
confirm worksheet deletion

' Delete the worksheet tab

Sheets("Pivot").Delete

Application.DisplayAlerts = True '       Reset
the default option on dialogue box that
confirms worksheet deletion

' Insert a blank tab after the last tab

Sheets.Add After:=Sheets(Sheets.Count)

Sheets(Sheets.Count).Name = "Pivot" ' Rename
the active tab"

Sheets("Pivot").Activate

' Place the cursor at cell A1 in order to
prepare for the search

Range("A1").Select

LastRowWithData =
```

```vba
Sheets("Rearranged").Columns(1).Find(What:="
*", SearchOrder:=xlByRows,
SearchDirection:=xlPrevious).Row ' Search
```
through the specified column in a backwards
direction from the current cursor position
and provides the row number which contains
the last row of text, then stores this row
number in the numeric variable called
LastRowWithData

' Create a pivot table on cell A3 of the
"Pivot" tab, which has its source data in
the "Clean Data" worksheet

```vba
ActiveWorkbook.PivotCaches.Create(SourceType
:=xlDatabase,
SourceData:="Rearranged!R1C1:R" &
LastRowWithData & "C3",
Version:=xlPivotTableVersion12).CreatePivotT
able TableDestination:="Pivot!R3C1",
TableName:="PivotTable1",
DefaultVersion:=xlPivotTableVersion12
```

' Insert Row Field

```vba
With
ActiveSheet.PivotTables("PivotTable1").Pivot
Fields("CustID")

    .Orientation = xlRowField

    .Position = 1

End With
```

```vba
'The period column is set up as a column

With
ActiveSheet.PivotTables("PivotTable1").Pivot
Fields("Day")

    .Orientation = xlColumnField

    .Position = 1

' Insert Value Fields

End With


ActiveSheet.PivotTables("PivotTable1").AddDa
taField
```

```
ActiveSheet.PivotTables("PivotTable1").Pivot
Fields("Amount ($)"), "Sum of Amount ($)",
xlSum

' This sub-routine removes all subtotals
from the pivot table using a more compact
and universal method than the regular macro
record method, which lists all values for
all variables.

Dim PivTbl2 As PivotTable

Dim PivFld2 As PivotField

On Error Resume Next

    For Each PivTbl2 In
Application.ActiveSheet.PivotTables

        For Each PivFld2 In
PivTbl.PivotFields

            PivFld2.Subtotals(1) = True

            PivFld2.Subtotals(1) = False

        Next

    Next

On Error GoTo 0
```

```vba
' Remove grand totals from columns but keep
them for rows

With ActiveSheet.PivotTables("PivotTable1")

    .ColumnGrand = False

    .RowGrand = True

End With

' Change pivot design to "Tabular"

ActiveSheet.PivotTables("PivotTable1").RowAx
isLayout xlTabularRow

' Format Pivot Table

ActiveSheet.PivotTables("PivotTable1").ShowT
ableStyleRowStripes = False

ActiveSheet.PivotTables("PivotTable1").Table
Style2 = "PivotStyleMedium9"
```

```vba
' DRAFT 4: Step 11

'            Select the default option on
dialogue box to confirm worksheet deletion

Application.DisplayAlerts = False

Sheets("Summary").Delete ' Delete the
worksheet tab

'     Reset the default option on dialogue
box that confirms worksheet deletion

Application.DisplayAlerts = True

'Dim LastRowPivot As Long ' Remove
apostrophe before Dim if the following
section of code is separated from the code
above

'Dim LastColumnPivot As Long' Remove
apostrophe before Dim if the following
section of code is separated from the code
above



'Determine the last row in the pivot table

With
ActiveSheet.PivotTables("PivotTable1").Table
Range1

    LastRowPivot =
Sheets("Pivot").UsedRange.Rows.Count

    LastColumnPivot =
Sheets("Pivot").UsedRange.Columns.Count

End With
```

```vba
' Insert a blank tab before the last tab

Sheets.Add Before:=Sheets(1)

Sheets(1).Name = "Summary" ' Rename the
active tab"

Sheets("Summary").Activate

Range("A1").Activate

Sheets("Pivot").Activate

Range(Cells(1, 1), Cells(LastRowPivot,
LastColumnPivot)).Select

Selection.Copy

Sheets("Summary").Activate

'Paste Values

Selection.PasteSpecial Paste:=xlPasteValues,
Operation:=xlNone, SkipBlanks:=False,
Transpose:=False

Application.CutCopyMode = False ' Remove
clipboard cut/copy border (aka "ants")

End Sub
```